SO-ADL-796

Stars

Lynn M. Stone

Rourke
Publishing LLC
Vero Beach, Florida 32964

© 2009 Rourke Publishing LLC

All rights reserved. No part of this book may be reproduced or utilized in any form or by any means, electronic or mechanical including photocopying, recording, or by any information storage and retrieval system without permission in writing from the publisher.

www.rourkepublishing.com

PHOTO CREDITS: All images © NASA; except page 4: © Soubrettepage; 10: © Derris Lanier; page 12: © konradlew; page 13: © Heintje Joseph Lee; page 18-19: © Iain Jaques;

Editor: Meg Greve

Cover and Interior designed by: Tara Raymo

Library of Congress Cataloging-in-Publication Data

Stone, Lynn M.
  Stars / Lynn Stone.
       p. cm. -- (Skywatch)
  Includes index.
  ISBN 978-1-60472-297-0
  1. Stars--Juvenile literature. I. Title.
  QB801.7.S73 2009
  523.8--dc22
                            2008024852

Printed in the USA

CG/CG

Table of Contents

stars

Look into a clear night sky and you wi
certainly see stars. They look like tiny,
twinkling lights.

4

There are so many stars in outer space, that we could never count them all!

5

are giant balls of **gas**. They a
ely hot and bright.

Loops of g
from the

Stars are made mostly of a gas called hydrogen.

7

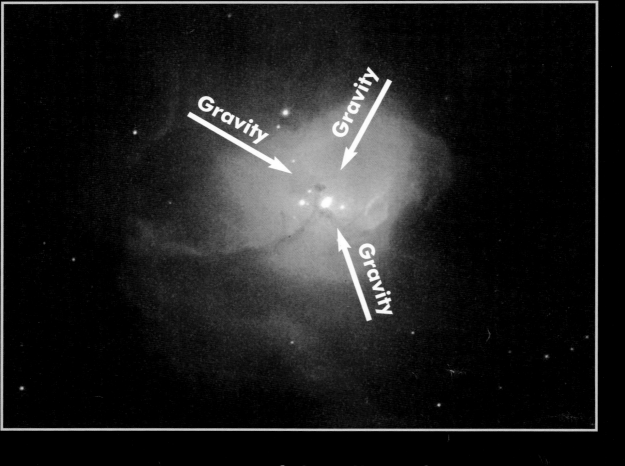

Gravity, a powerful pulling force, holds together the gases that form stars.

The Closest Star

Most stars are billions of miles away from Earth. One star, the Sun, is much closer to Earth than any other. The Sun is about 93 million miles (149 million kilometers) from Earth.

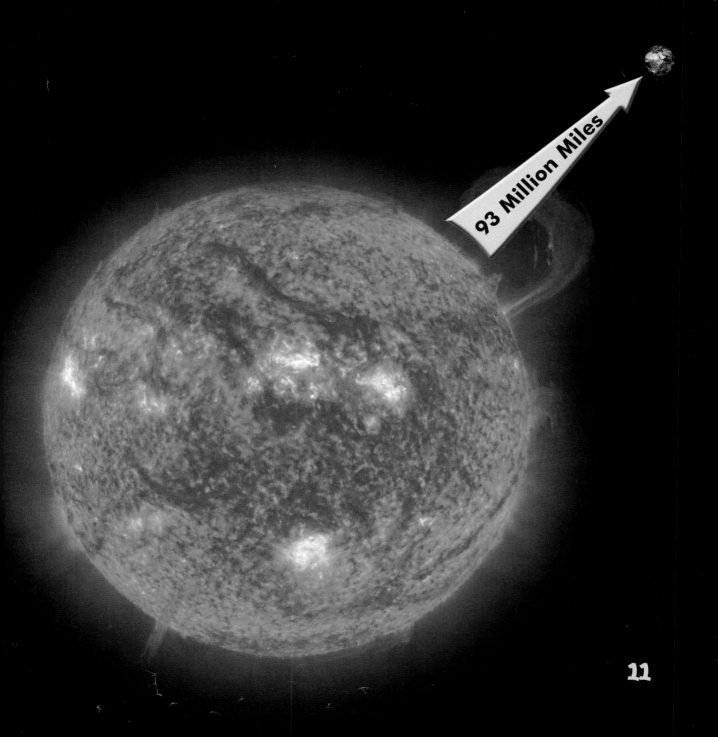

93 Million Miles

11

We see the Sun during the day and all of the other stars at night. This does not mean they are not shining. The glare of the sunlight makes the other stars too **dim** to be seen.

Day

Night

13

Different Kinds of Stars

Stars change over millions of years. They become smaller as their gases lose their energy.

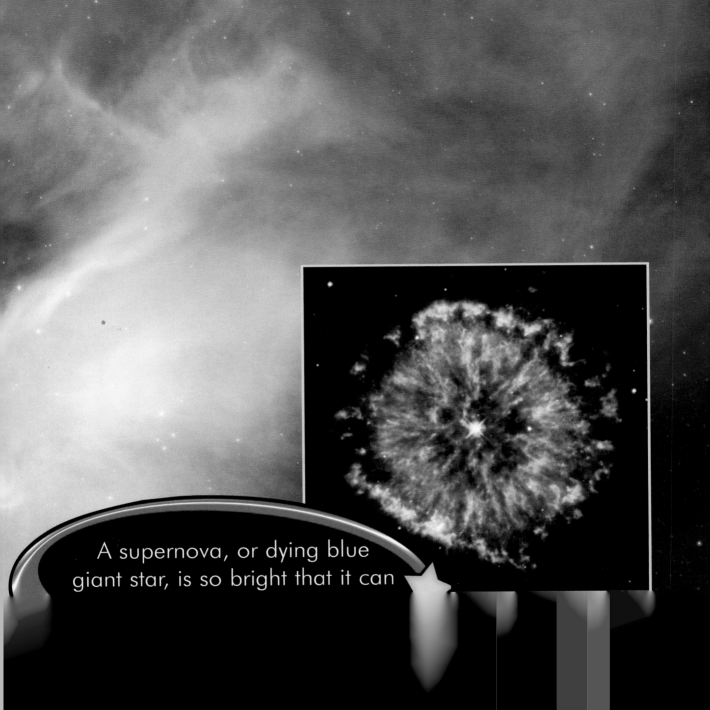

A supernova, or dying blue
giant star, is so bright that it can

Stars can be different ages, sizes, temperatures, brightness, and colors. Cooler stars appear to be red, while hotter stars might be blue or white.

Astronomers look through special filters on a telescope to see the colors of a star.

At times, you might see what we call a shooting or falling star. These streaks of light are not really stars, but **meteoroids** burning up in our **atmosphere**.

Meteoroid

19

The Milky Way

The stars that we can see make up the **Milky Way**. It is a group of more than 100 billion stars. The Milky Way is the **galaxy** in which we live.

The Milky Way is one of billions of galaxies.

No one knows the exact number of galaxies in our universe. Scientists are sure that there are billions to be discovered!

Glossary

atmosphere (AT-muhss-fihr): the mixture of gases that surround a planet

dim (DIM): not bright

galaxy (GAL-uhk-see): a group of several billion stars

gas (GASS): matter such as air that is not a liquid or a solid

gravity (GRAV-uh-tee): a powerful physical force that tends to pull objects toward it

meteoroids (MEE-tee-uh-roids): small pieces of rock or debris in the solar system

Milky Way (MILK-ee WAY): the visible galaxy of which our solar system is a part

Index

Further Reading

Twist, Clint. *Stars*. School Specialty Publishing, 2006.

Mitchell, Melanie S. *Sun*. Lerner, 2004.

Bingham, Caroline. *First Space Encyclopedia*. DK Publishing, 2008.

Websites to Visit

http://hubblesite.org/the_telescope/hubble_essentials/

http://www.frontiernet.net/~kidpower/astronomy.html

www.astronomy.com/stars.htm

http://www.esq.int/esakIDSen/starsandgalaxies.html

About the Author

Lynn M. Stone is a widely-published wildlife and domestic animal photographer and the author of more than 500 children's books. His book *Box Turtles* was chosen as an Outstanding Science Trade Book and Selectors' Choice for 2008 by the Science Committee of the National Science Teachers' Association and the Children's Book Council.